Contents

D1364727

Why Critical Thinking?

The Problem:

Everyone thinks; it is our nature to do so. But much of our thinking, left to itself, is biased, distorted, partial, uninformed or down-right prejudiced. Yet the quality of our life and that of what we produce, make, or build depends precisely on the quality of our thought. Shoddy thinking is costly, both in money and in quality of life. Excellence in thought, however, must be systematically cultivated.

A Definition:

Critical thinking is the art of analyzing and evaluating thinking with a view to improving it.

The Result:

A well cultivated critical thinker:

- raises vital questions and problems, formulating them clearly and precisely;
- gathers and assesses relevant information, using abstract ideas to interpret it effectively;
- comes to well-reasoned conclusions and solutions, testing them against relevant criteria and standards;
- thinks openmindedly within alternative systems of thought, recognizing and assessing, as need be, their assumptions, implications and practical consequences; and
- communicates effectively with others in figuring out solutions to complex problems.

Critical thinking is, in short, self-directed, self-disciplined, self-monitored and self-corrective thinking. It requires rigorous standards of excellence and mindful command of their use. It entails effective communication and problem solving abilities and a commitment to overcoming our native egocentrism and sociocentrism.

The Elements of Thought

Point of View
frames of reference,
perspectives,
orientations

Purpose
goals,
objectives

Implications and Consequences

Question at issue
problem, issue

Elements of Thought

Assumptions
presuppositions,
axioms, taking for
granted

Information
data, facts, reasons,
observations,
experiences,
evidence

Concepts
theories,
definitions, laws,
principles, models

Interpretation and Inference
conclusions,
solutions

Used With Sensitivity to Universal Intellectual Standards

Clarity → Accuracy → Depth → Breadth → Significance
Precision   ↓
Relevance   Fairness

A Checklist for Reasoning

1) All reasoning has a PURPOSE.

- Can you state your purpose clearly?
- What is the objective of your reasoning?
- Does your reasoning focus throughout on your goal?
- Is your goal realistic?

2) All reasoning is an attempt to figure something out, to settle some QUESTION, to solve some PROBLEM.

- What question are you trying to answer?
- Are there other ways to think about the question?
- Can you divide the question into sub-questions?
- Is this a question that has one right answer or can there be more than one reasonable answer?
- Does this question require judgment rather than facts alone?

3) All reasoning is based on ASSUMPTIONS.

- What assumptions are you making? Are they justified?
- How are your assumptions shaping your point of view?
- Which of your assumptions might reasonably be questioned?

4) All reasoning is done from some POINT OF VIEW.

- What is your point of view? What insights is it based on? What are its weaknesses?
- What other points of view should be considered in reasoning through th problem? What are the strengths and weaknesses of these viewpoints? Are you fairmindedly considering the insights behind these viewpoints

All reasoning is based on DATA, INFORMATION, and EVIDENCE.

- To what extent is your reasoning supported by relevant data?
- Do the data suggest explanations that differ from those you have given?
- How clear, accurate, and relevant are the data to the question at issue?
- Have you gathered data sufficient to reaching a reasonable conclusion?

All reasoning is expressed through, and shaped by, CONCEPTS and THEORIES.

- What key concepts and theories are guiding your reasoning?
- What alternative explanations might be possible, given these concepts and theories?
- Are you clear and precise in using concepts and theories in your reasoning?
- Are you distorting ideas to fit your agenda?

All reasoning contains INFERENCES or INTERPRETATIONS by which we draw CONCLUSIONS and give meaning to data.

- To what extent do the data support your conclusions?
- Are your inferences consistent with each other?
- Are there other reasonable inferences that should be considered?

All reasoning leads somewhere or has IMPLICATIONS and CONSEQUENCES.

- What implications and consequences follow from your reasoning?
- If we accept your line of reasoning, what implications or consequences are likely?

Questions Using the Elements of Thought

(in a paper, an activity, a reading assignment...)

Purpose:
What am I trying to accomplish?
What is my central aim? My purpose?

Questions:
What question am I raising?
What question am I addressing?
Am I considering the complexities in the question?

Information:
What information am I using in coming to that conclusion?
What experience have I had to support this claim?
What information do I need to settle the question?

Inferences/ Conclusions:
How did I reach this conclusion?
Is there another way to interpret the information?

Concepts:
What is the main idea here?
Can I explain this idea?

Assumptions:
What am I taking for granted?
What assumption has led me to that conclusion?

Implications/ Consequences:
If someone accepted my position, what would be the implications?
What am I implying?

Points of View:
From what point of view am I looking at this issue?
Is there another point of view I should consider?

Three Levels of Thought

Level 3:
Highest Order Thinking
- Explicitly reflective
- Highest skill level
- Routine use of critical thinking tools in analyzing and assessing thinking
- Consistently fair

Level 2:
Higher Order Thinking
- Selectively reflective
- High skill level
- Lacks critical thinking vocabulary
- Inconsistently fair, may be skilled in sophistry

Level 1:
Lower Order Thinking
- Unreflective
- Low to mixed skill level
- Frequently relies on gut intuition
- Largely self-serving/ self-deceived

Lower order thinking is often distinguished from higher order thinking. But higher order thinking can be inconsistent in quality. It can be fair or unfair. To think at the highest level of quality, we need not only intellectual skills, but intellectual traits as well.

Universal Intellectual Standards:

And questions that can be used to apply them

Universal intellectual standards are standards which should be applied to thinking to ensure its quality. To be learned they must be taught explicitly. The ultimate goal, then, is for these standards to become infused in the thinking of students, forming part of their inner voice, guiding them to reason better.

Clarity:

Could you elaborate further on that point? Could you express that point in another way? Could you give me an illustration? Could you give me an example?

Clarity is a gateway standard. If a statement is unclear, we cannot determine whether it is accurate or relevant. In fact, we cannot tell anything about it because we don't yet know what it is saying. For example, the question "What can be done about the education system in America?" is unclear. In order to adequately address the question, we would need to have a clearer understanding of what the person asking the question is considering the "problem" to be. A clearer question might be "What can educators do to ensure that students learn the skills and abilities which help them function successfully on the job and in their daily decision-making?"

Accuracy:

Is that really true? How could we check that? How could we find out if that is true?

A statement can be clear but not accurate, as in "Most dogs weigh more than 30 pounds."

Precision:

Could you give me more details? Could you be more specific?

A statement can be both clear and accurate, but not precise, as in "Jack is overweight." (We don't know how overweight Jack is, one pound or 500 pounds.)

Relevance:

How is that connected to the question? How does that bear on the issue?

A statement can be clear, accurate, and precise, but not relevant to the question at issue. For example, students often think that the amount of effort they put into a course should be used in raising their grade in a course. Often, however, "effort" does not measure the quality of student learning, and when that is so, effort is irrelevant to their appropriate grade.

Depth:

How does your answer address the complexities in the question? How are you taking into account the problems in the question? Are you dealing with the most significant factors?

A statement can be clear, accurate, precise, and relevant, but superficial (that is, lack depth). For example, the statement "Just Say No", which was used for a number of years to discourage children and teens from using drugs, is clear, accurate, precise, and relevant. Nevertheless, those who use this approach treat a highly complex issue, the pervasive problem of drug use among young people, superficially. It fails to deal with the complexities of the issue.

Breadth:

Do we need to consider another point of view? Is there another way to look at this question? What would this look like from a conservative standpoint? What would this look like from the point of view of…?

A line of reasoning may be clear, accurate, precise, relevant, and deep, but lack breadth (as in an argument from either the conservative or liberal standpoints which gets deeply into an issue, but only recognizes the insights of one side of the question).

Logic:

Does this really make sense? Does that follow from what you said? How does that follow? Before you implied this and now you are saying that, I don't see how both can be true.

When we think, we bring a variety of thoughts together into some order. When the combination of thoughts are mutually supporting and make sense in combination, the thinking is "logical." When the combination is not mutually supporting, is contradictory in some sense, or does not "make sense," the combination is "not logical."

Fairness:

Are we considering all relevant viewpoints in good faith? Are we distorting some information to maintain our biased perspective? Are we more concerned about our vested interests than the common good?

We naturally think from our own perspective, from a point of view which tends to privilege our position. Fairness implies the treating of all relevant viewpoints alike without reference to one's own feelings or interests. Because we tend to be biased in favor of our own viewpoint, it is important to keep the standard of fairness at the forefront of our thinking. This is especially important when the situation may call on us to see things we don't want to see, or give something up that we want to hold onto.

Clarity	Could you elaborate further? Could you give me an example? Could you illustrate what you mean?
Accuracy	How could we check on that? How could we find out if that is true? How could we verify or test that?
Precision	Could you be more specific? Could you give me more details? Could you be more exact?
Relevance	How does that relate to the problem? How does that bear on the question? How does that help us with the issue?
Depth	What factors make this a difficult problem? What are some of the complexities of this question? What are some of the difficulties we need to deal with?
Breadth	Do we need to look at this from another perspective? Do we need to consider another point of view? Do we need to look at this in other ways?
Logic	Does all this make sense together? Does your first paragraph fit in with your last? Does what you say follow from the evidence?
Significance	Is this the most important problem to consider? Is this the central idea to focus on? Which of these facts are most important?
Fairness	Do I have any vested interest in this issue? Am I sympathetically representing the viewpoints of others?

Template for Analyzing the Logic of an Article

Take an article that you have been assigned to read for class, completing the "logic" of it using the template below. This template can be modified for analyzing the logic of a chapter in a textbook.

The Logic of "(name of the article)"

) The main purpose of this article is _____.
(State as accurately as possible the author's purpose for writing the article.)

) The key question that the author is addressing is _____.
(Figure out the key question in the mind of the author when s/he wrote the article.)

) The most important information in this article is _____.
(Figure out the facts, experiences, data the author is using to support her/his conclusions.)

) The main inferences/conclusions in this article are _____.
(Identify the key conclusions the author comes to and presents in the article.)

) The key concept(s) we need to understand in this article is (are)
_____. By these concepts the author means _____.
(Figure out the most important ideas you would have to understand in order to understand the author's line of reasoning.)

) The main assumption(s) underlying the author's thinking is (are)
_____. (Figure out what the author is taking for granted [that might be questioned].)

a) If we take this line of reasoning seriously, the implications are
_____. (What consequences are likely to follow if people take the author's line of reasoning seriously?)

b) If we fail to take this line of reasoning seriously, the implications are
_____. (What consequences are likely to follow if people ignore the author's reasoning?)

) The main point(s) of view presented in this article is (are)_____.
(What is the author looking at, and how is s/he seeing it?)

Criteria for Evaluating Reasoning

1. **Purpose:** What is the purpose of the reasoner? Is the purpose clearly stated or clearly implied? Is it justifiable?

2. **Question:** Is the question at issue well-stated? Is it clear and unbiased? Does the expression of the question do justice to the complexity of the matter at issue? Are the question and purpose directly relevant to each other?

3. **Information:** Does the writer cite relevant evidence, experiences, and/or information essential to the issue? Is the information accurate? Does the writer address the complexities of the issue?

4. **Concepts:** Does the writer clarify key concepts when necessary? Are the concepts used justifiably?

5. **Assumptions:** Does the writer show a sensitivity to what he or she is taking for granted or assuming? (Insofar as those assumptions might reasonably be questioned?) Does the writer use questionable assumptions without addressing problems which might be inherent in those assumptions?

6. **Inferences:** Does the writer develop a line of reasoning explaining well how s/he is arriving at her or his main conclusions?

7. **Point of View:** Does the writer show a sensitivity to alternative relevant points of view or lines of reasoning? Does s/he consider and respond to objections framed from other relevant points of view?

8. **Implications:** Does the writer show a sensitivity to the implications and consequences of the position s/he is taking?

Intellectual
Integrity

Intellectual
Autonomy

Intellectual
Humility

Intellectual
Empathy

*Intellectual
Traits or Virtues*

Confidence
in Reason

Intellectual
Courage

Intellectual
Perseverance

Fairmindedness

Essential Intellectual Traits

Intellectual Humility   vs Intellectual Arroganc

Having a consciousness of the limits of one's knowledge, including a sensitivity to circumstances in which one's native egocentrism is likely to function self-deceptively, sensitivity to bias, prejudice and limitations of one's viewpoint. Intellectual humility depends on recognizing that one should not claim more than one actually knows. It does not imply spinelessness or submissiveness. It implies the lack of intellectual pretentiousness, boastfulness, or conceit, combined with insight into the logical foundations, or lack of such foundations, of one's beliefs.

Intellectual Courage   vs Intellectual Cowardic

Having a consciousness of the need to face and fairly address ideas, beliefs or viewpoints toward which we have strong negative emotions and to which we have not given a serious hearing. This courage is connected with the recognition that ideas considered dangerous or absurd are sometimes rationally justified (in whole or in part) and that conclusions and beliefs inculcated in us are sometimes false or misleading. To determine for ourselves which is which, we must not passively and uncritically "accept" what we have "learned." Intellectual courage comes into play here, because inevitably we will come to see some truth in some ideas considered dangerous and absurd, and distortion or falsity in some ideas strongly held in our social group. We need courage to be true to our own thinking in such circumstances. The penalties for nonconformity can be severe.

Intellectual Empathy   vs Intellectual Narrow-mindednes

Having a consciousness of the need to imaginatively put oneself in the place of others in order to genuinely understand them, which requires the consciousness of our egocentric tendency to identify truth with our immediate perceptions of long-standing thought or belief. This trait correlates with the ability to reconstruct accurately the viewpoints and reasoning of others and to reason from premises, assumptions, and ideas other than our own. This trait also correlates with the willingness to remember occasions when we were wrong in the past despite an intense conviction that we were right, and with the ability to imagine our being similarly deceived in a case-at-hand.

Intellectual Autonomy   vs Intellectual Conformity

Having rational control of one's beliefs, values, and inferences. The ideal of critical thinking is to learn to think for oneself, to gain command over one's thought processes. It entails a commitment to analyzing and evaluating beliefs on the basis of reason and evidence, to question when it is rational to question, to believe when it is rational to believe, and to conform when it is rational to conform.

Intellectual Integrity   vs Intellectual Hypocrisy

Recognition of the need to be true to one's own thinking; to be consistent in the intellectual standards one applies; to hold one's self to the same rigorous standards of evidence and proof to which one holds one's antagonists; to practice what one advocates for others; and to honestly admit discrepancies and inconsistencies in one's own thought and action.

Intellectual Perseverance   vs Intellectual Laziness

Having a consciousness of the need to use intellectual insights and truths in spite of difficulties, obstacles, and frustrations; firm adherence to rational principles despite the irrational opposition of others; a sense of the need to struggle with confusion and unsettled questions over an extended period of time to achieve deeper understanding or insight.

Confidence In Reason   vs Distrust of Reason and Evidence

Confidence that, in the long run, one's own higher interests and those of humankind at large will be best served by giving the freest play to reason, by encouraging people to come to their own conclusions by developing their own rational faculties; faith that, with proper encouragement and cultivation, people can learn to think for themselves, to form rational viewpoints, draw reasonable conclusions, think coherently and logically, persuade each other by reason and become reasonable persons, despite the deep-seated obstacles in the native character of the human mind and in society as we know it.

Fairmindedness   vs Intellectual Unfairness

Having a consciousness of the need to treat all viewpoints alike, without reference to one's own feelings or vested interests, or the feelings or vested interests of one's friends, community or nation; implies adherence to intellectual standards without reference to one's own advantage or the advantage of one's group.

Three Kinds of Questions

In approaching a question, it is useful to figure out what type it is. Is it a question with one definitive answer? Is it a question that calls for a subjective choice? Or does the question require you to consider competing points of view?

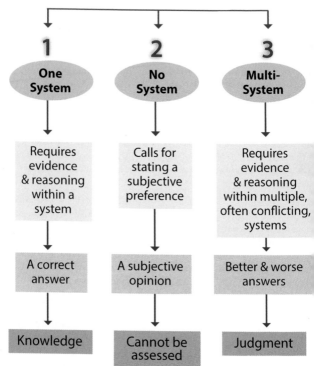

A Template for Problem-Solving

To be an effective problem solver:

) Figure out, and regularly re-articulate, your goals, purposes, and needs. Recognize problems as obstacles to reaching your goals, achieving your purposes, or satisfying your needs.

) Wherever possible take problems one by one. State each problem as clearly and precisely as you can.

) Study the problem to determine the "kind" of problem you are dealing with. For example, what do you have to do to solve it?

) Distinguish problems over which you have some control from problems over which you have no control. Concentrate your efforts on problems you can potentially solve.

) Figure out the information you need to solve the problem. Actively seek that information.

) Carefully analyze and interpret the information you collect, drawing reasonable inferences.

) Determine your options for action. What can you do in the short term? In the long term? Recognize your limitations in terms of money, time, and power.

• Evaluate your options, determining their advantages and disadvantages.

• Adopt a strategy. Follow through on it. This may involve direct action or a carefully thought-through wait-and-see approach.

) When you act, monitor the implications of your action. Be ready to revise your strategy if the situation requires it. Be prepared to change your analysis or statement of the problem, as more information about the problem becomes available.

Analyzing & Assessing Research

Use this template to assess the quality of any research project or paper

1) All research has a fundamental PURPOSE and goal.
   - Research purposes and goals should be clearly stated.
   - Related purposes should be explicitly distinguished.
   - All segments of the research should be relevant to the purpose.
   - All research purposes should be realistic and significant.
2) All research addresses a fundamental QUESTION, problem or issue.
   - The fundamental question at issue should be clearly and precisely stated.
   - Related questions should be articulated and distinguished.
   - All segments of the research should be relevant to the central question.
   - All research questions should be realistic and significant.
   - All research questions should define clearly stated intellectual tasks that, being fulfilled
     settle the questions.
3) All research identifies data, INFORMATION, and evidence relevant to its fundamental
   question and purpose.
   - All information used should be clear, accurate, and relevant to the fundamental
     question at issue.
   - Information gathered must be sufficient to settle the question at issue.
   - Information contrary to the main conclusions of the research should be explained.
4) All research contains INFERENCES or interpretations by which conclusions are drawn.
   - All conclusions should be clear, accurate, and relevant to the key question at issue.
   - Conclusions drawn should not go beyond what the data imply.
   - Conclusions should be consistent and reconcile discrepancies in the data.
   - Conclusions should explain how the key questions at issue have been settled.
5) All research is conducted from some POINT OF VIEW or frame of reference.
   - All points of view in the research should be identified.
   - Objections from competing points of view should be identified and fairly addressed.
6) All research is based on ASSUMPTIONS.
   - Clearly identify and assess major assumptions in the research.
   - Explain how the assumptions shape the research point of view.
7) All research is expressed through, and shaped by, CONCEPTS and ideas.
   - Assess for clarity the key concepts in the research.
   - Assess the significance of the key concepts in the research.
8) All research leads somewhere (i.e., has IMPLICATIONS and consequences).
   - Trace the implications and consequences that follow from the research.
   - Search for negative as well as positive implications.
   - Consider all significant implications and consequences.

Critical thinkers routinely apply intellectual standards to the elements of reasoning in order to develop intellectual traits.

THE STANDARDS

Clarity	Precision
Accuracy	Significance
Relevance	Completeness
Logicalness	Fairness
Breadth	Depth

Must be applied to

THE ELEMENTS

Purposes	Inferences
Questions	Concepts
Points of view	Implications
Information	Assumptions

As we learn to develop

INTELLECTUAL TRAITS

Intellectual Humility	Intellectual Perseverance
Intellectual Autonomy	Confidence in Reason
Intellectual Integrity	Intellectual Empathy
Intellectual Courage	Fairmindedness

Stages of Critical Thinking Development

Accomplished Thinker
(Intellectual skills
and virtues have
become second
nature in our lives)

Advanced Thinker
(We are committed to lifelong
practice and are beginning to
internalize intellectual virtues)

Practicing Thinker
(We regularly practice and
advance accordingly)

Beginning Thinker
(We try to improve but
without regular practice)

Challenged Thinker
(We are faced with significant
problems in our thinking)

Unreflective Thinker
(We are unaware of significant
problems in our thinking)

The Problem of Egocentric Thinking

Egocentric thinking results from the unfortunate fact that humans do not naturally consider the rights and needs of others. We do not naturally appreciate the point of view of others nor the limitations in our own point of view. We become explicitly aware of our egocentric thinking only if trained to do so. We do not naturally recognize our egocentric assumptions, the egocentric way we use information, the egocentric way we interpret data, the source of our egocentric concepts and ideas, the implications of our egocentric thought. We do not naturally recognize our self-serving perspective.

As humans we live with the unrealistic but confident sense that we have fundamentally figured out the way things actually are, and that we have done this objectively. We naturally believe in our intuitive perceptions—however inaccurate. Instead of using intellectual standards in thinking, we often use self-centered psychological standards to determine what to believe and what to reject. Here are the most commonly used psychological standards in human thinking.

"IT'S TRUE BECAUSE I BELIEVE IT." Innate egocentrism: I assume that what I believe is true even though I have never questioned the basis for many of my beliefs.

"IT'S TRUE BECAUSE WE BELIEVE IT." Innate sociocentrism: I assume that the dominant beliefs of the groups to which I belong are true even though I have never questioned the basis for those beliefs.

"IT'S TRUE BECAUSE I WANT TO BELIEVE IT." Innate wish fulfillment: I believe in whatever puts me (or the groups to which I belong) in a positive light. I believe what "feels good," what does not require me to change my thinking in any significant way, what does not require me to admit I have been wrong.

"IT'S TRUE BECAUSE I HAVE ALWAYS BELIEVED IT." Innate self-validation: I have a strong desire to maintain beliefs that I have long held, even though I have not seriously considered the extent to which those beliefs are justified by the evidence.

"IT'S TRUE BECAUSE IT IS IN MY SELFISH INTEREST TO BELIEVE IT." Innate selfishness: I believe whatever justifies my getting more power, money, or personal advantage even though these beliefs are not grounded in sound reasoning or evidence.

The Problem of Sociocentric Thinking

Most people do not understand the degree to which they have uncritically internalized the dominant prejudices of their society or culture. Sociologists and anthropologists identify this as the state of being "culture bound." This phenomenon is caused by sociocentric thinking, which includes:

- The uncritical tendency to place one's culture, nation, religion above all others.

- The uncritical tendency to select self-serving positive descriptions of ourselves and negative descriptions of those who think differently from us.

- The uncritical tendency to internalize group norms and beliefs, take on group identities, and act as we are expected to act—without the least sense that what we are doing might reasonably be questioned.

- The tendency to blindly conform to group restrictions (many of which are arbitrary or coercive).

- The failure to think beyond the traditional prejudices of one's culture.

- The failure to study and internalize the insights of other cultures (improving thereby the breadth and depth of one's thinking).

- The failure to distinguish universal ethics from relativistic cultural requirements and taboos.

- The failure to realize that mass media in every culture shapes the news from the point of view of that culture.

- The failure to think historically and anthropologically (and hence to be trapped in current ways of thinking).

- The failure to see sociocentric thinking as a significant impediment to intellectual development.

Sociocentric thinking is a hallmark of an uncritical society. It can be diminished only when replaced by cross-cultural, fairminded thinking — critical thinking in the strong sense.

Envisioning Critical Societies

> The critical habit of thought, if usual in society, will pervade all its mores, because it is a way of taking up the problems of life. Men educated in it cannot be stampeded by stump orators ... They are slow to believe. They can hold things as possible or probable in all degrees, without certainty and without pain. They can wait for evidence and weigh evidence, uninfluenced by the emphasis or confidence with which assertions are made on one side or the other. They can resist appeals to their dearest prejudices and all kinds of cajolery. Education in the critical faculty is the only education of which it can be truly said that it makes good citizens.
>
> William Graham Sumner, 1906

Humans have the capacity to be rational and fair. But this capacity must be developed. It will be significantly developed only if critical societies emerge. Critical societies will develop only to the extent that:

- Critical thinking is viewed as essential to living a reasonable and fairminded life.
- Critical thinking is routinely taught; consistently fostered.
- The problematics of thinking are an abiding concern.
- Closed-mindedness is systemically discouraged; open-mindedness systematically encouraged.
- Intellectual integrity, intellectual humility, intellectual empathy, confidence in reason, and intellectual courage are social values.
- Egocentric and sociocentric thinking are recognized as a bane in social life.
- Children are routinely taught that the rights and needs of others are equal to their own.
- A multi-cultural world view is fostered.
- People are encouraged to think for themselves and discouraged from uncritically accepting the thinking or behavior of others.
- People routinely study and diminish irrational thought.
- People internalize universal intellectual standards.

If we want critical societies we must create them.

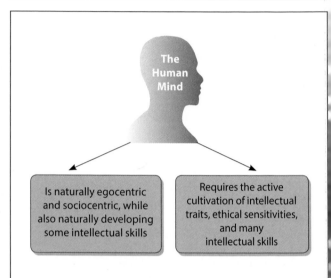

Essential Idea: Humans have a natural tendency, all other things being equal, to make decisions and to reason egocentrically or sociocentrically. Humans also have (largely undeveloped) rational capacities. Humans begin life as primarily egocentric creatures. Over time, infantile egocentric self-centered thinking merges with sociocentric group-centered thinking. All humans regularly engage in both forms of irrational thought. The extent to which any of us is egocentric or sociocentric is a matter of degree and can change significantly in given situations or contexts. While egocentric and sociocentric propensities are naturally occurring phenomena, rational capacities must be largely developed. It is through the development of these rational capacities that we combat irrational tendencies and cultivate critical societies.